Flippers and Fins ™

Swimming with Penguins

Miriam Coleman

PowerKiDS press

New York

Published in 2010 by The Rosen Publishing Group, Inc.
29 East 21st Street, New York, NY 10010

First Edition

Editor: Joanne Randolph
Book Design: Greg Tucker
Photo Researcher: Jessica Gerweck

Photo Credits: Cover Frank Krahmer/Getty Images; p. 5 Kim Heacox/Getty Images; p. 7 Ralph Lee Hopkins/Getty Images; p. 9 Andy Rouse/Getty Images; p. 11 © Paul Souders/Corbis; pp. 13, 21 John Giustina/Getty Images; p. 15 John Eastcott and Yva Momatiuk/Getty Images; p. 17 Bill Curtsinger/Getty Images; p. 19 Doug Allen/Getty Images.

Library of Congress Cataloging-in-Publication Data

Coleman, Miriam.
  Swimming with penguins / Miriam Coleman. — 1st ed.
    p. cm. — (Flippers and fins)
  Includes index.
  ISBN 978-1-4042-8094-6 (library binding) — ISBN 978-1-4358-3245-9 (pbk.) — ISBN 978-1-4358-3246-6 (6-pack)
  1. Penguins—Juvenile literature. I. Title.
  QL696.S473C654 2010
  598.47—dc22

                              2008055825

Manufactured in the United States of America

Contents

Meet the Penguin

A parade of birds marches across an icy field. With black coats and white chests, they look like they are dressed for a party. They **waddle** on their short little legs. When the birds tire of walking, they hop onto their fat stomachs and slide across the ice. These birds are penguins.

Penguins are sometimes called feathered fish because they cannot fly and they spend so much time in the water. Their bodies are shaped so that they can swim quickly through the water. In fact, penguins are such good swimmers that early **explorers** to **Antarctica** once mistook them for fish.

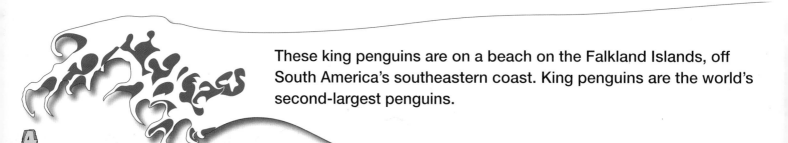

These king penguins are on a beach on the Falkland Islands, off South America's southeastern coast. King penguins are the world's second-largest penguins.

Where Penguins Live

Penguins live on every **continent** in the Southern Hemisphere, the part of the world that lies south of the **equator**. They live on islands near New Zealand and Australia, on the coasts of South America and southern Africa, and on Antarctica. Different **species**, or kinds, of penguins prefer different **climates**. The emperor penguin and Adélie penguin live only in icy Antarctica. Galápagos penguins live under the hot sun of the equator.

Penguins spend most of their lives swimming in the sea. When they come on land to raise their young, they form huge groups, called colonies. Some colonies include millions of penguins.

To live on the hot equator, Galápagos penguins, like these, have fewer, looser feathers than other penguins so that they can get rid of extra heat more easily.

Kinds of Penguins

There are 17 different species of penguins. All penguins have dark backs and light fronts. Some penguins, like the emperor and king penguins, also have orange and yellow feathers on their heads and chests. The beaks, or bills, of different species can be black, red, purple, or orange. Penguin feet can be black, blue, orange, or pink.

The largest species of penguin is the emperor penguin. The emperor stands about 4 feet (1 m) tall and weighs up to 100 pounds (45 kg). The smallest penguin is called a fairy penguin. It can grow to be 1 foot (30 cm) tall and weighs only about 3 pounds (1 kg).

Macaroni penguins live in Antarctica and on islands off South America and Africa. They are known for the yellow or orange feathers on their heads.

Flippers or Wings?

Penguins are birds, but they cannot fly. Penguins' wings are too small to lift their heavy bodies into the air. Instead, a penguin's wings have adapted, or changed, over time to become flippers.

A penguin's flippers are built for swimming and diving. The bones inside their flippers are flat and wide, making a shape like a paddle. Over the bones are powerful muscles, which move the penguin through the water. The flippers are covered with very short feathers, which are almost like fish scales. Underwater, the penguin moves its flippers as other birds move their wings. This makes it look as though the penguin is flying through the water.

Here some king penguins look for food under water. King penguins use their long flippers to dive as deep as 1,640 feet (500 m) to find food.

Diving In

Penguins may look funny on land, but under water, they move like **torpedoes**. Emperor penguins are the fastest species of penguin. They can reach nearly 9 miles per hour (14 km/h).

Penguins are not fish, so they must breathe air like all other birds. Most penguins come up to breathe at least once a minute.

Sometimes penguins must dive to find food that lives deep in the ocean. Chinstrap penguins can dive down as far as 230 feet (70 m) below the surface, or top of the water. Emperor penguins can dive down over 1,700 feet (518 m) down.

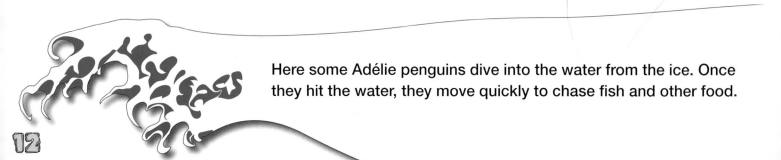

Here some Adélie penguins dive into the water from the ice. Once they hit the water, they move quickly to chase fish and other food.

Staying Warm

Penguins that live in cold places have many tricks for keeping warm. They can **huddle** together to use each other's body heat. They can shiver and hold their flippers close to their bodies. Penguins also have a thick layer of fat called blubber to keep them warm.

A penguin's thick coat of feathers is its best tool for fighting the cold. The top feathers are oily, which makes them waterproof. A bottom coat of soft, downy feathers keeps the penguin warm. Penguins spend a lot of time cleaning their feathers and keeping them in place. At least once a year, penguins will molt, or shed all of their feathers. The old feathers get worn down, so penguins need to grow a whole new set.

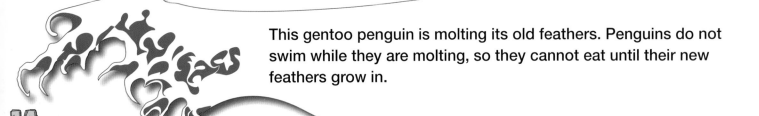

This gentoo penguin is molting its old feathers. Penguins do not swim while they are molting, so they cannot eat until their new feathers grow in.

Catching Dinner

Penguins need to eat a lot because they use up so much **energy** swimming. They eat fish, squid, and crustaceans, which are shelled animals such as shrimp and crabs. Penguins find all of their food in the sea. They catch their food and swallow it whole while they swim. Penguins spend most of their lives in the water looking for food. They come ashore when it is time to mate.

Sometimes penguins have to fast, or go without food. They fast while they watch their nests on land and when they shed their feathers to grow new ones. Before fasting, they build up a layer of blubber on which they live.

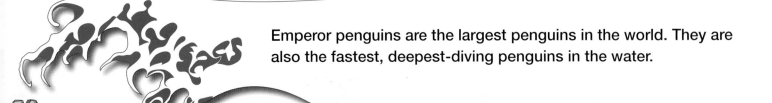

Emperor penguins are the largest penguins in the world. They are also the fastest, deepest-diving penguins in the water.

Hatching Chicks

When penguins are ready to **breed**, they come ashore and form colonies. Most penguins build nests out of stones or feathers. The parents take turns keeping the eggs warm through an unfeathered piece of skin on their stomachs, called a brood patch.

After a month or two, the eggs hatch. Penguin chicks are born with soft feathers. The two parents keep their babies warm under their brood patches. They take turns hunting for food and **regurgitating** it for the chick. Once the chick grows its waterproof feathers, it can leave its parents and head into the sea.

Emperor and king penguins do not build nests. Instead the father holds the egg on his feet, keeping it warm under his brood patch.

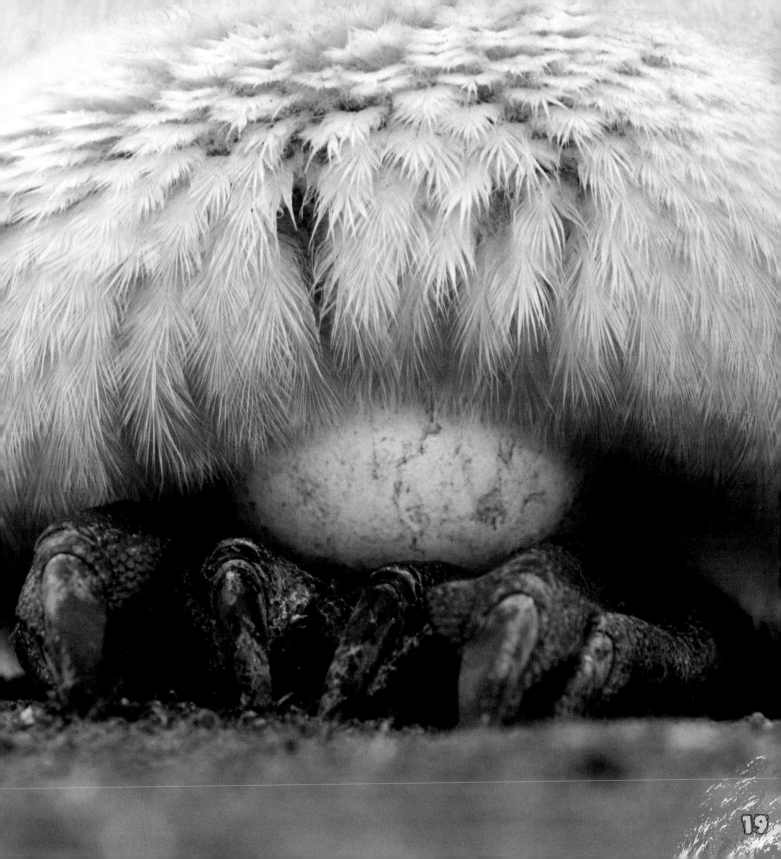

A Closer Look: Adélie Penguins

When most people picture penguins, they think of the Adélie penguin. Adélies were named for the wife of a French explorer. With more than two million breeding pairs, Adélie penguins are the most common penguins in Antarctica. They also breed farther south than any other penguin. To reach their breeding grounds, Adélies travel a long way, sometimes crossing 50 miles (80 km) of sea ice.

Adélies are small penguins. They stand about 27.5 inches (70 cm) tall and weigh between 8.5 and 12 pounds (4–5 kg). Adélie penguins are good jumpers and can leap up to 6.5 feet (2 m) in the air. This helps them leap over the cliffs of ice around the sea where they live.

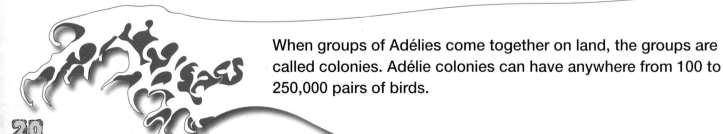

When groups of Adélies come together on land, the groups are called colonies. Adélie colonies can have anywhere from 100 to 250,000 pairs of birds.

A Bird of Extremes

Life is not always easy for penguins. They must travel far to breed and eat. They can die if they get too cold in a storm or they can be eaten by leopard seals.

People can also put penguins in danger. Oil spills can hurt their feathers and make it hard for penguins to keep warm. Overfishing in their waters can take away their food.

Penguins are strong little animals, though. They live in a wider range of climates than any other birds. From hot, **tropical** shores to icy Antarctic waters, penguins have made themselves at home in **extreme** places.

Glossary

Antarctica (ant-AHRK-tih-kuh) The icy land at the southern end of Earth.

breed (BREED) To make babies.

climates (KLY-mits) The kinds of weather certain places have.

continent (KON-tuh-nent) One of Earth's seven large landmasses.

energy (EH-nur-jee) The power to work or to act.

equator (ih-KWAY-tur) The imaginary line around Earth that separates it into two parts, northern and southern.

explorers (ek-SPLOR-erz) People who travel and look for new land.

extreme (ik-STREEM) Going past the expected or common. Extreme weather might be very hot or very cold.

huddle (HUH-dul) To crowd together.

regurgitating (re-GUR-juh-tayt-ing) Throwing up partly eaten food.

species (SPEE-sheez) A single kind of living thing. All people are one species

torpedoes (tor-PEE-dohz) Underwater missiles that move quickly through the water and blow up when they hit something.

tropical (TRAH-puh-kul) Having to do with the warm parts of Earth that are near the equator.

waddle (WAH-del) To walk slowly while rocking from side to side.

Index

Web Sites

Due to the changing nature of Internet links, PowerKids Press has developed an online list of Web sites related to the subject of this book. This site is updated regularly. Please use this link to access the list:

www.powerkidslinks.com/ffin/penguin/